THE MAGIC OF GOAL SETTING *getting*

How to transform your results with GALAHAD - the Simple 7-Step Action-Taking System

Gill Smith

The Business Wizard

The Business Kitchen Spearhead System

The Magic of Goal Getting - How to transform your results with GALAHAD - the Simple 7-Step Action Taking System | 1st Edition

ISBN - 978-1-5272-8675-7 (Paperback Edition)

All diagrams copyright The Business Kitchen
Typesetting and design by ASR Creative Communications

Published by The Business Kitchen, Gloucester, England

www.thebusinesskitchen.net

ACKNOWLEDGEMENTS

To Peter Thomson and all his team for their help, support and inspiration that gave me the confidence to share my ideas in this book.

To Sue Portman at ASR Creative Communications for her expertise and eye for design and for bearing with me as things changed.

And to all the dedicated small business owners across Gloucestershire who continue to be the heart of business in the county.

FOREWORD

Goals and targets and plans and visions and missions and…

The list goes on and on.

But how the heck do I get the 'stuff' done that gets the 'stuff' done?

That is the question. And one that's puzzled and frustrated and balded many a budding entrepreneur or even experienced achiever.

Now, at last, here's Gill Smith and her simply brilliant (and brilliantly simple) GALAHAD process.

It works. I know, I've used it. It's simple (not always easy of course) and it works.

Clear direction achieved. Actions noted. Progress recorded. Happiness – at last.

If you've ever struggled to set goals that mean something to you (personal or business). If you've wandered off track (hasn't everyone?). If you've even given up and later regretted that decision…

Now you have the answers in the palm of your hand.

This book should be supplied to every student, every business bank account opener, every manager, every leader and certainly every coach or consultant.

Please, I urge you – take this opportunity to learn and apply Gill's wisdom. For that's what it is. Not merely information or instruction, but pure distilled wisdom.

I am so glad I did.

Peter Thomson

Peter Thomson
"The World's Most Prolific Information Product Creator"

Contents

CHAPTER 1

My Lightbulb Moment

And then, I suddenly realised what was missing in the process…

As a trainer, I find that it is very easy, too easy, to make assumptions about people's ability to actually get things done.

When the The Business Kitchen started in 2014, we created a membership called *The Main Course*, offering face-to-face group training. A key part of each session was creating 30-day action plans.

At the end of every monthly workshop each member drew up their own plan. The aim was to help them achieve the next milestone on the way towards their 3-year aspirational goal. Sharing this with the other members introduced a level of accountability and commitment.

In fact, accountability was an integral part of the training programme. At the following month's meeting, each member updated us on progress against the plan.

Disappointingly often, none was made as there 'hadn't been enough time' or 'there was too much else to do'. Clearly the process I was sharing had some fatal flaws and wasn't delivering the value I knew it was able to. This needed to be remedied!

After trying several different ways of handling that part of the meeting, I found the missing piece.

And so, GALAHAD was born – a simple to follow 7 step process you can use time and time again for any action plan related to any goal.

> *"The value of an idea lies in the using of it."*
>
> Thomas Edison

CHAPTER 2

Why this book is for you

This book is for you if you never quite get around to creating action plans. Or the plans you create are seldom delivered because everything else gets in the way and time disappears.

Let me ask you a question. *Are you running your business – or is your business running you?*

Does your working day end with a sigh of satisfaction – or a groan of despair that you haven't done all the 'stuff' you meant to do when you started out that morning? And is this particularly true for the tasks aimed at working 'on' the business?

Your goals and objectives are often forgotten in the rush of 'busy-ness' that is a normal working day. But after a while, you start losing sight of your 'why' – and that wears you down. Without a defining purpose, your business becomes no more than a 'job'. And I doubt that's what you were aiming for when you began.

Perhaps you end up feeling frustrated, exhausted, guilty, angry, or all of these?

This is not the freedom and choice you probably wanted from your business! And it can seem as though there is no way to change it.

Well, the good news is that my 7 step GALAHAD process can help you ACE your planning. You'll create and implement the action plans that will set up a great future for your business and put you on the path to achieving your personal goals.

This book is not about time management although some elements of good practice are included.

GALAHAD is the accumulation of everything I have learned about creating action plans that work. It comes from my years working on large projects in the corporate world, from setting up and running my own businesses, and training other business owners. I believe that if something can be systemised, then it should be. It takes away all the guess work, all the starting from scratch and provides a reliable method to achieve an outcome. GALAHAD has been tried and tested by many different businesses in many different industries. They all agree it has changed how they approach action planning.

WHAT YOU GO AWAY WITH

Follow the steps in this book and go away with a simple, easy to follow and repeatable process that helps you create effective action plans, every time.

The system is called GALAHAD which stands for:

- **G**oals
- **A**ctivities
- **L**ogical order
- **A**ssign
- **H**ow Long
- **A**llocate
- **D**iarise

Along with these 7 steps there is one other that is essential. It's covered in Chapter 11.

WHAT YOU NEED BEFORE YOU GET STARTED

Preparation is key to everything.

The very first thing to do is to download the workbook by going to: **http://bit.ly/galahadworkbook** or scan the QR code on page 80.

Make sure you have gathered or done everything on the Preparation checklist in the workbook.

Preparation

Description	✓
A commitment to following the process and putting in the time	
An open mind	
A clear space on your desk	
Turn off all notifications from social media and emails	
Turn off your phone or set to silent	
A comfortable office chair	
Good lighting	
This book	
A pen and notebook or a computer and electronic document	
Lots of post-it notes	
Some large sheets of blank paper (A3 or larger)	

The Preparation checklist is on page 3 of the GALAHAD Workbook

HOW TO USE THIS BOOK

Each activity in the book has a corresponding template in the accompanying workbook. You can either print the workbook or complete online – the choice is entirely yours. The workbook can be used time and time again and the online templates allow you to build up the plan without the constraints of the printed page.

All my templates are simply suggestions that match the principles of each activity. If you prefer a different format then go for it. Perhaps mindmaps work best for you or you prefer to use images rather than words. Use whatever format works for you. Just make sure you follow the principles and the individual steps.

THE ICONS

I have included icons throughout the book to flag activities or important points. They are:

Note
An interesting note or signpost

Key Point
A critical point that can affect your success

Activity
What it says on the tin - there's work to do

Warning
Danger points to look for and beware of

Tip
A useful piece of information that will help you use GALAHAD effectively

"Great things are done by a series of small things brought together."

Vincent Van Gogh

CHAPTER 3

What is an Action Plan?

For the purposes of this book I am defining an Action Plan as a structured list of the key things that need to happen to move your business forward and achieve your goals. The focus is working 'on' your business, rather than 'in' it.

Let's first think about what makes a good action plan. In summary it has the following characteristics:

- A clear statement of what needs to be done. It has a date, responsible person and the resources needed to perform each activity
- The desired outcome is defined in a SMART goal format (more of that later)
- The outcome will deliver benefit or improvement, or mitigate a risk or issue
- The outcome can be measured in terms of its effect
- It consists of a set of activities that need to be performed to achieve the desired outcome

Why is an action plan different from a 'To do' list?

A 'To Do' list may include some clearly defined actions but will likely:

a) be longer

b) be less measurable and

c) will include items that are more aide memoire than a true value-delivering action

It is easy for the activities from your action plan and the tasks from your To Do list to get mixed up, leaving you feeling overwhelmed, confused and discombobulated. So later in this book I will share some techniques for preventing this. Employ these and the overlap should be a thing of the past (once these techniques become a habit).

If you have a clear immediate goal and need to get an action plan set up urgently, then go to Chapter 5 and get started straight away.

"Plan your work and work your plan."

Napoleon Hill

CHAPTER 4

G is for Goals

Before we can start taking action we need to know where we are trying to get to. The greater clarity we have on our goals the more effective our actions will be.

In *The 7 Habits of Highly Successful People* Stephen Covey wrote "If the ladder is not leaning against the right wall, every step we take just gets us to the wrong place faster"!

So, we want to make sure the ladder is leaning against the right wall (for where we are now - the wall can and will change).

I don't know about you, but goal setting is often harder than it feels it ought to be. People say 'set your goals' as though it is the simplest thing in the world and sometimes it isn't. It is so easy to set goals that are either much less than you want, less than you are capable of. And even easier to get caught up worrying about the 'how' rather than the goal's result.

Sometimes we are frightened to set the goals we want because others may criticise them. Sometimes the pressure from others causes us to set goals that are what they expect even though these are not what is important to us. Goals are often expressed as financial targets. But it is seldom all about the money. It is more to do with what money we need to live the life we want to live, and the life we want for others.

The important thing when setting your goals is that they are truly what you want.

If your goals are about achieving success, are you clear on your own definition? What does success look like to you?

For me success is having the freedom to do what I want and to help the people I want to help, without being constrained by finances or time or mindset.

This book focuses on your business, but it is important that you set your business goals within the context of your definition of success.

With the business owners I work with, I help them define the mission and vision for their businesses. Have you done this for your business?

And what about setting your personal mission statement? Have you decided on what my friend Peter Johnson would call the 'Rules of My Game'? Your personal mission statement is your philosophy or your creed. Who do you want to be and what do you want to do?

For example, your personal mission might include things such as always being honest; performing a random act of kindness each day; working in a methodical and focused way or delivering what you promise.

Take one of your large pieces of paper and copy the diagram on the right. In each of the spaces add in all your words and thoughts that describe how you would like to be living in the future. There are some questions on page 4 of the workbook to prompt you.

Don't worry about the 'how' or whether you can achieve a goal. Do you remember how as a child you would daydream about doing all sorts of things, unrestricted by experience or self-belief? Nothing was impossible. When setting your goals, aim to be in that state of mind.

PASTIMES & INTERESTS
:
COMMUNITY
:   VALUES
•   •
•   •
•   •
•

MY LIFE

HEALTH & WELLNESS
•   FAMILY & FRIENDS
•   •
•   •

PHYSICAL ENVIRONMENT
•
•
•

My Life possible questions are on page 4 of the GALAHAD Workbook

---

COMMUNITY
• My goal is to help through donation and connections and to donate expertise to one local charity on a regular basis

PASTIMES & INTERESTS
• My goal is to spend 5 weeks a year exploring the UK and for the business to be only 4 days a week and never on weekends.
• I want to explore English history and walk the south coast path and the coast to coast and to learn another language.

VALUES
• My values are honesty, integrity, generosity and commitment
• I want to be known as a leading authority in my field.
• My goal is to live each day in line with my values and to help as many people as I can with a random act of kindness every day

HEALTH & WELLNESS
• My goal is to swim every day, to get 7 hours sleep per night; to meditate daily and to work with a personal trainer to improve fitness and strength.
• To study for a masters degree

MY LIFE

FAMILY & FRIENDS
• My goal is to spend time with friends every week and to create shared memories.
• To phone regularly and to share holidays each year.

FINANCE AND INCOME
• My goal is to have a monthly income of £10,000 to allow me to be financially secure, enjoy leisure time and help others as needed

PHYSICAL ENVIRONMENT
• My goal is to live in a 4 bed house 10 minutes from the ocean and to have a library, swimming pool and a garden office.
• The property would be private but not isolated and would have views and there would be a Mercedes GLA sitting on the drive.

Having mapped out your personal goals and mission it's time to think about your business goals. What does your business need to deliver? What does it need to look like to support your dreams and your definition of success?

To do this I use a tool called the **Vision Roadmap**. It lays out where you are aiming for, where you are starting from and the main milestones along the way.

Turn to the next template in the workbook and take the following steps below to complete your own Vision Roadmap

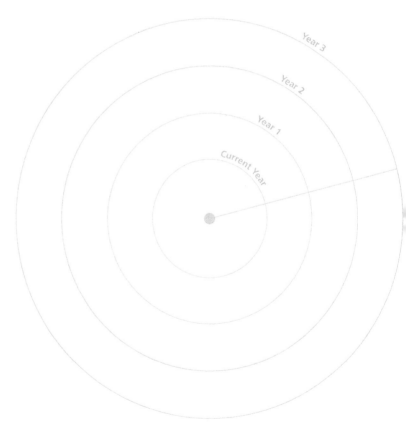

The blank Vision Roadmap template is on page 5 of the GALAHAD Workbook

The spokes are the components of your business. The four I always start with are:

- Turnover – absolute or additional
- Customers – for example type, number, or mix
- Markets – perhaps location or industry
- Products or services – could be number, mix or type

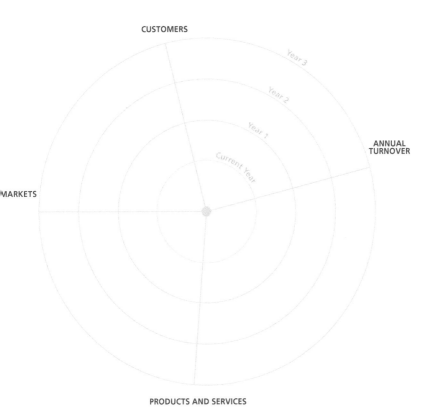

For each spoke decide on the 3-year goal.

The goal should follow the SMART principles attributed to Peter Drucker's 'Management by Objectives' concept.

S is for Specific so write the goal in a way that gives total clarity. For example, 'Increase the number of customers' is too general. Improve it by changing to 'Increase my customer numbers by 5'.

M is for Measurable so that it's easy to determine whether the goal has been achieved. If it hasn't, what was the under or over delivery? To be measurable you need a clear idea of what effect the outcome of the goal has. For my example above, how will you measure the new customers generated as a direct result of the action taken? If you can't measure it, you can't manage it, and you can't improve the effectiveness of the actions.

A is for Achievable. The goal needs to be something you feel is possible, but it should also be aspirational. If it makes you feel a little bit scared about whether you can do it then it is probably set at about the right level. Setting a goal that feels much too 'pie in the sky' is one of the big mistakes people make. On the other hand, setting a goal that is really easy to reach will reduce the feeling of achievement. So, the goal needs to be achievable (to keep you believing) but aspirational (to challenge you).

R is for Relevant. In the original Peter Drucker list, the R was for Realistic. It seems to me that there is little difference between 'realistic' and 'achievable', so I use 'Relevant' instead. The goal needs to be relevant to the longer-term picture.

T is for Timely. Your goal needs to be targeted for achievement by a certain date. It needs a time limit on it. In this book I focus on 30 day plans so the time boundary for any goal on your plan would be 30 days from the starting date of the plan. Are your goals going to take longer? No problem, chunk them down into smaller milestones and include those.

DO NOT worry about how you will achieve it!

"Remember 'some' is not a number and 'soon' is not a time."

Anon

STEP 3 – Current status

Now complete the current status by putting in today's numbers or status. You need to know where you are starting from before you can decide on what actions to take

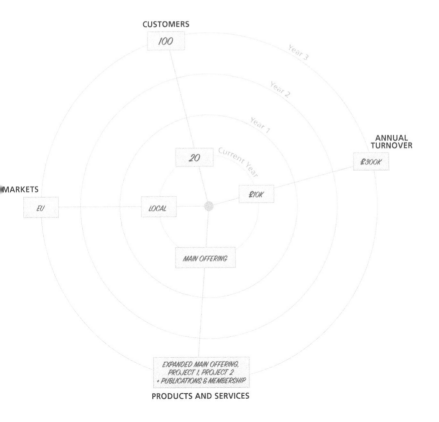

STEP 4 – Intervening values

Add in the intervening values for Year 1 and Year 2. I recommend you keep this simple and just use a straight-line approach.

For example, your 3-year turnover goal is £300k, and you're starting at £10k. At the end of year 2 you'd aim for £200k. At the end of the first year, £100k. There might only be a small gap between your start point and your year 1 target as you build up.

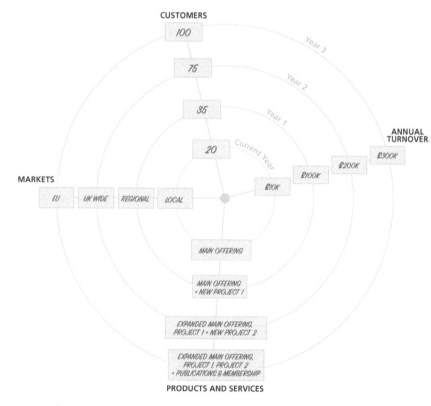

This Vision Roadmap example is on page 6 of the GALAHAD Workbook

You can extend the Vision Roadmap to include more components of your business. This might include hours spent in the business each week, margin levels, profit, number of employees, location, premises or products etc.

The example below shows an anonymised version from one of my members. They used their Vision Roadmap to help them keep on track strategically. If, for example, a new piece of equipment caught their eye they would take a look at the Vision Roadmap and see whether the machinery helped move them towards the 3-year goal. If it didn't, they would either review and amend the goal or refrain from going ahead with the purchase.

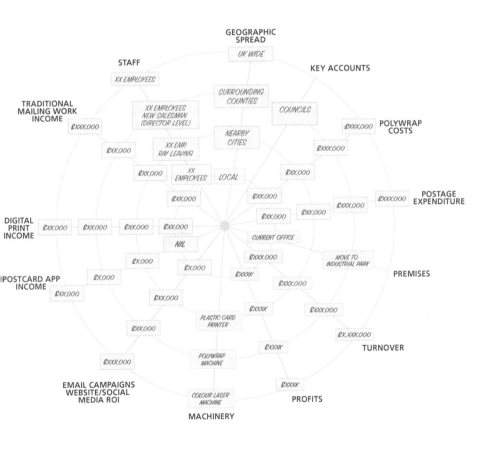

KEY POINTS

Start with the desired 3-year outcome, then mark the current position. Finally, fill in the intervening information.

Remember to create the business goals within the context of your life goals. (It is worth doing the My Life exercise with your partner or family). Revisiting this may give you some of the spokes that you want to include on the Vision Roadmap for the business.

Now pick the most important spoke – the one that has the most impact in terms of moving your business towards the bigger goals TODAY!

The action plans created by following GALAHAD aim to move the strategy of your business forward. So, the goals you set need to be relevant to your business vision, mission, and overall aims. That way, you're climbing the *right* ladder.

Before you map out the actions you need to take to deliver the goal there are a few more preparatory steps.

STEP 5 – What do you need?

The next question you need to ask yourself is 'have I got all the things I need to achieve the goal?' Or to achieve the first milestone at least. This will include skills, knowledge, equipment, experts, software, or materials. Missing anything? What will you do to get it?

It may be easy to decide what the measure is. But what are the mechanics to measure the results? Is it five new appointments in your diary? An uplift in the bank account? A new salesperson hitting targets every month?

Or is it less obvious? This may mean there are more activities needed in support of the goal.

– What data do you need to create and capture?

– Where will the data come from?

– Will you measure success by a survey or feedback form?

A top tip is to write down your goal and read it regularly. This will increase the probability of you achieving it. Always write goals in the present tense (as though they have already been achieved).

Later in the book I look at some tips and techniques for keeping on track (Chapter 12).

> *"The more boundless your vision, the more real you are."*
>
> **Deepak Chopra**

CHAPTER 5

A is for Activities

The first 'A' of GALAHAD is for 'Activities'.

But wait!

Before we dive into the detail, we must first split our long-term goals into shorter milestones.

For example, the Year 1 goal for turnover from the Vision Roadmap is £100k. You're starting from £10k, so you're seeking an extra £90k by year end. Using a very simple approach, the goal for 6 months time would be to add £45k. For 90 days it would be £22,500 and for 30 days time it would be an additional £7,500.

This approach makes the action planning more straightforward. It often helps make the goal feel much more possible because what needs to be achieved is a smaller chunk.

If the goal is about increasing your team size, then the first milestone might be preparing and agreeing the job specification. (See the examples at the back of the book of how to split down the different types of spoke.)

I recommend writing down the 90-day goal and then setting out Milestone 1 (end of 30 days) and Milestone 2 (end of 60 days). Working with my members, I have found that it gives more context to the 30-day goal. 90 days is long enough to get some major 'work on the business' activities completed but not so long it ends up encouraging 'I'll do it tomorrow'. Of course, it does also depend on how important the goal is to you!

90 Day Planning Template

VISION ROADMAP SPOKE: **Date:**
3 YEAR GOAL:
1-year milestone:
6-month milestone:
90-day milestone:
MONTH 1: Milestone 1 What outcome needs to be reached by end of month 1 to be on track for 90-day goal?
MONTH 2: Milestone 2 What outcome needs to be reached by end of month 2 to be on track for 90-day goal?
MONTH 3: 90 Day Milestone What outcome needs to be reached by end of month 3 to reach 90-day goal?

Complete the 90-day template. Make sure Milestone 1 and 2 are also defined as SMART goals. Once you have defined Milestone 1, you can start working on the detailed activities.

This 90 Day Planning template is on page 7 of the GALAHAD Workbook

90 Day Planning Example

VISION ROADMAP SPOKE: Turnover	Date: 1 Sep 20

3 YEAR GOAL:

£290,000 extra

1-year milestone:

£90,000 extra

6-month milestone:

£45,000 extra

90-day milestone:

£22,500 extra

MONTH 1: Milestone 1

What outcome needs to be reached by end of month 1 to be on track for 90-day goal?

Onboard 3 clients at a monthly revenue of £2500 each and generate 10 leads to convert to clients in October

---

MONTH 2: Milestone 2

What outcome needs to be reached by end of month 2 to be on track for 90-day goal?

Onboard 3 clients at a monthly revenue of £2500 each and generate 10 leads to convert to clients in November

---

MONTH 3: 90 Day Milestone

What outcome needs to be reached by end of month 3 to reach 90-day goal?

Onboard 3 clients at a monthly revenue of £2500 each and generate 10 leads to convert to clients in December

Starting with your 30-day milestone you can now break down all the tasks needed to achieve it. So the next thing to do is:

List the activities at a very detailed level.

For example, having an activity such as 'update the website' is too high level. It might involve writing copy, collecting images, testing the customer journey, or deciding on layout before you physically update the website.

The more granular you are the better. Detailed activities make it easier to delegate to others. It is also easier to estimate how long things are going to take as there is less risk of missing 'hidden' things. Breaking actions down into individual, smaller steps will make it much easier to do the 'first' thing.

 I recommend using post-it notes for the next few steps in the system but you can use a sheet of paper. If you do, then space out the activities so there is room to add other information between them as you go through the process.

 Take a pack of post-it notes and write down all the things that need to be done to achieve Milestone 1. Put each one on a separate post-it note.

List them as you think of them. Don't worry about the order or who is going to do them as this may get in the way of capturing all your thoughts.

Once you have listed all the activities you can think of; review them. Check they are relevant to the goal you are focusing on. In my experience it is so easy for random activities from the 'To Do' list and other goals to get added in unintentionally!

Create a parking lot for any that don't belong. Your parking lot can be a reminder list on your PC, in a notebook, or on a whiteboard. Don't forget to have a process for reviewing this on a regular basis so ideas and actions don't get lost.

> "But remember, dreams without goals are just dreams and they ultimately fuel disappointment. So, have dreams but have goals – life goals, yearly goals, monthly goals, daily goals. To achieve you need discipline; consistency EVERY day; plan EVERY day... Hard work works. Don't confuse movement with progress."
>
> **Denzel Washington**

The 7 Step Action Planning System to Achieve Any Goal ■

CHAPTER 6

L is for Logical Order

Before you can put together the final action plan you need to work out the order of the activities. Depending on how you think, you may have written down the activities in the logical order, so this step will be very easy!

Take each of the activities and work out the logical order by sorting the post-it notes (or writing the number against each on your piece of paper).

What is the very first thing that needs to happen? Double check there is nothing that needs to happen before this. That makes sure nothing is missed. If there is, create another activity. Check that there are no leaps of faith between activities too!

The most likely place for there to be missing activities is right at the beginning of the logical flow. For example, the first activity might be 'Write email copy' but this can't be done if there is no clarity on the audience, the required outcome, the offering etc. So, it maybe there are some other preparatory activities needed before 'Writing the email copy' can happen.

What preparation needs to be completed before each activity? What does each activity need to have ready to get started?

Once you have the post-it notes in order I recommend numbering them. Then if they get shuffled it doesn't matter. (And you can use the reference numbers for the next steps to save writing the activity description more than once.)

It is important to review the logical order and to check that each activity is adding value before the next step. Here is a tool to help you check this out.

Put your activities into logical order

On the Task Planner template, write the reference numbers from the post-it notes or piece of paper, in order, in the left-hand column. Then complete the 'outcome' column for each activity. Ask yourself 'What does this activity produce once it is done?'. Does each activity have a clear outcome, a reason for being there?

The outcome from one activity should be the starting point for the next one. Do you need to add in any missing activities? Create and add into the sequence.

Do you have any activities where there is no clear outcome? These can often be eliminated from the plan without affecting achievement of the goal.

Defining the outcome(s) of each activity will also help with the later review step.

Activities may have more than one outcome.

For example, if the activity is 'make 5 follow up calls' then you might identify 4 possible outcomes:

1. They answer the phone and the conversation goes ahead as planned
2. They answer the phone, but it is not a convenient time
3. They don't answer the phone and the call goes to voice mail
4. The number is unobtainable

Do you have a clear process for each of these possibilities? And for the action plan, what activity needs to follow on? And have you included it?

The Task Planner

Activity Number	OUTCOME	Next Activity

This Task Planner template is on page 8 of the GALAHAD Workbook

Below is an example of the Task Planner filled in using the example post-it notes from page 32. As you can see, there can be several different outcomes from an activity.

The Task Planner

Activity Number	OUTCOME	Next Activity
1	Confirmed list of 20 prospects to be targeted	2
2	Copy for email written	3
3	Mailchimp campaign set up	4
4	Mailchimp campaign sent	5, 6 or 8
5	Follow up calls for 'open not booked' made	6
6	Sales conversations completed	7
7	Clients onboarded	End
8	Follow up campaign sent to non – openers	6

"Logic takes care of itself; all we have to do is to look and see how it does it."

Ludwig Wittgenstein

CHAPTER 7

A is for Assign

The second 'A' of GALAHAD is for 'Assign' which is about how you can create more capacity by having some activities done by others.

Sir John Harvey Jones is attributed with saying *'Only do what only you can do'.*

So, an important part of the process is to decide which of the activities YOU have to do and which could be done by others. There are two types of activity where this makes sense. The first and most obvious is where you simply don't know how to do it. The second is where you don't want to do it, even though you could.

I know, from working with many businesses, that people find this quite hard to do. There are all sorts of reasons given – some are around control and trust, some are around cash, and some are around just not knowing how.

Even if you decide not to delegate, it's still worth looking at the activities and assessing your *Skills, Knowledge, Desire (SKD) Index.* Your SKD Index will highlight the activities you could or should be delegating to other experts. The starting point here is that you are probably doing everything at the moment. That isn't going to work longer term if you want to grow the business.

Remember to look at whether any of the activities can be automated. Create a separate plan for getting that done.

🔲🔲

This is not recommended but IF you are totally convinced that there is no way anything that needs doing can be given to someone else, then leap to Chapter 8. Simply write your own name in the 'Delegate' column on the template.

🔲🔲

STEP 1 – Identify the skills and knowledge needed for each activity

Assigning Template

Activity Number	Skills	Knowledge	Proficiency	Desire	SKD Indicator	Opportunity Cost	Delegate Y/N	Resource

The Assigning template is on page 9 of the GALAHAD Workbook

Using the activity reference numbers from either the post-it notes or the piece of paper write this into the template. Against each, write down what skills and knowledge are needed to perform that activity competently and to the standard required. One way to think about this is to imagine that you had to write this as part of a job specification.

For example, the activity might be 'Compile confirmed list of 20 prospects'.

The skills or knowledge needed to perform this would include knowing where to get the data from, how to select it and handling the results.

Skills and Knowledge

Activity Number	Skills	Knowledge	Proficiency	Desire	SKD Indicator	Opportunity Cost	Delegate Y/N	Resource
1	Data manipulation PC use	Hubspot filtering Sales funnel status values Which targets are best bet?						

Don't worry too much about whether what is needed is classified as a skill or knowledge.

STEP 2 Rate your proficiency

In the next column, rate how good you are at performing the activity where 10 is 'Nail it every single time' and 1 is 'I really shouldn't be let anywhere near it'!

I generally find that most business owners are at least a '6' on most activities as they have had to develop some level of competency to have got as far as they have.

Proficiency

Activity Number	Skills	Knowledge	Proficiency	Desire	SKD Indicator	Opportunity Cost	Delegate Y/N	Resource
1	Data manipulation PC use	Hubspot filtering Sales funnel status values Which targets are best bet?	8					

STEP 3 Assess your desire

In the next column assess your desire for doing the activity where '10' is 'Absolutely love it' and 1 is 'If I never had to do it again it would be too soon'.

This is where you can start identifying the actions you could and should be delegating now or in the future.

Desire

Activity Number	Skills	Knowledge	Proficiency	Desire	SKD Indicator	Opportunity Cost	Delegate Y/N	Resource
1	Data manipulation PC use	Hubspot filtering Sales funnel status values Which targets are best bet?	8	4				

STEP 4 Assess whether you should be performing the activity

The final part is to think about whether you **should** be the one to complete the activity. Just because you love doing something does not necessarily mean you should!

There are two factors that can help you decide whether an activity could/should be delegated. The first is the SKD indicator and the second the financial value, or opportunity cost.

Use my SKD indicator to get you started.

Take the 'Proficiency' and the 'Desire' scores from the previous steps, decide whether you can delegate the task, and look up your SKD indicator on the table below.

SKD Index Matrix

Your Proficiency Score	Your Desire score	Can you delegate?	SKD Indicator
Less than or equal to 7	Less than or equal to 7	Yes	B
Less than or equal to 7	Less than or equal to 7	No	C/D
Less than or equal to 7	Greater than 7	Yes	B
Less than or equal to 7	Greater than 7	No	C/D
Greater than 7	Less than or equal to 7	Yes	A
Greater than 7	Less than or equal to 7	No	C/D
Greater than 7	Greater than 7	Yes	A
Greater than 7	Greater than 7	No	C/D

Score each item as follows:

- *A - Yes: you absolutely should be performing the activity; you are the ONLY one who can do it (today and in the future).*

- *B - Yes: you absolutely should be performing the activity; you are the ONLY one who can do it (today and in the future). BUT you need to invest in some training to increase your proficiency*

- *C - you absolutely should not be doing the activity and you can delegate immediately*

- *D – you absolutely should not be doing the activity but that can't happen until later*

SKD Indicator

Activity Number	Skills	Knowledge	Proficiency	Desire	SKD Indicator	Opportunity Cost	Delegate Y/N	Resource
1	Data manipulation PC use	Hubspot filtering Sales funnel status values Which targets are best bet?	8	4	C			

For those marked D – 'Later', annotate with a target date for delegating the task. Develop an action plan to make it happen.

Now you have a view of the activities you should consider delegating or where you need to invest in some training.

The final factor to help with deciding is to consider the financial factor - the opportunity cost. Here's a true story about a company whose turnover was £2m per annum. The CEO was still collecting and sorting the post every day. When their true role was defined and valued, it showed up an opportunity cost of around £200 per hour! That's an expensive postman.

What is the value of your time? How much revenue would you otherwise generate in the time spent on the activity? And are you clear what the revenue generation activities are in your business?

I understand it may not be possible to delegate all the things you would like immediately. Identifying future opportunities is an important part of your strategy (your future operating model).

Step 5 Fill in the opportunity cost column on the sheet

Opportunity Cost

Activity Number	Skills	Knowledge	Proficiency	Desire	SKD Indicator	Opportunity Cost	Delegate Y/N	Resource
1	Data manipulation PC use	Hubspot filtering Sales funnel status values Which targets are best bet?	8	4	C	£200		

Step 6 Decide whether the activity can/should be delegated

Delegation

Activity Number	Skills	Knowledge	Proficiency	Desire	SKD Indicator	Opportunity Cost	Delegate Y/N	Resource
1	Data manipulation PC use	Hubspot filtering Sales funnel status values Which targets are best bet?	8	4	C	£200	Y	

Step 7 Fill in the resourcing column

Who/what type of person should be doing the activity for this current action plan?

Resource

Activity Number	Skills	Knowledge	Proficiency	Desire	SKD Indicator	Opportunity Cost	Delegate Y/N	Resource
1	Data manipulation PC use	Hubspot filtering Sales funnel status values Which targets are best bet?	8	4	C	£200	Y	Virtual Assistant

There are many sources and types of resource to help with different activities. These are listed in Resourcing Activities on page 67. I am sure you can think of some others.

In the early days of a business cash may be tight, so it can be tricky to ask others to undertake some of the activities. Look at other ways of 'paying' for experts such as skill swaps, interns, or using low priced alternatives such as Fiverr.

One of the key things to look at is whether a process step is really one thing. Can it be split further into smaller steps that could be resourced differently?

I like to describe this activity as **'upskilling the business'**.

It's all about having the *right* person, with the *right* skills, performing the *right* role.

HOW DO YOU FIND THE RIGHT PEOPLE?

Start by making sure you understand exactly what you're asking for. You won't be able to communicate the results you want if you haven't got it clear in your mind first.

Have total clarity on the brief for the role or the service. This should include their responsibilities and the expected quality and delivery time. What outcomes do you want? What if they don't deliver? For an employee you would write a job description and the principle is the same for hiring anyone to do anything in your business. Think about having probationary or trial periods. If it is not working then it is easier to terminate the arrangement.

Do the research. Understand enough about the areas to be able to evaluate the candidates or service provider. Speak to others you know who can give you pointers on what you should be asking. Ask for evidence behind their promises. Don't be too impressed by certificates and qualifications. Certificates do not an expert make.

Be sure to get references. If your prospective supplier has not been personally recommended (or probably even if they have) ask for two or three references and speak to one or two of them before appointing. If the solution is another business – are they happy for you to talk to one or more of their existing clients? Unless they are in an industry where security doesn't allow this, then why would they not let you speak to existing clients? Make sure you have a clear idea of what you want to ask the referee. When you get recommendations make sure you get a clear picture of what the prospective supplier/employee delivered for the person making the recommendation. Is it relevant to what you are looking for?

Interview any possible supplier and make sure they are going to be someone you get on with and have the right personality.

Think about the first contact. Did it feel professional and competent? Are you happy for them to represent your brand?

Where the solution is another business did they ask you about your customers, your ethos, your values, your offer, and your long-term goals?

Have clear Terms and Conditions, even for informal arrangements. It will save hassle in the longer term if anything goes wrong and will minimise the risk of miscommunication.

- **Abdicating not delegating.** Be they employee or supplier they are representing your brand. Have the appropriate supervisory controls in place and look at what skills you might need to be effective in this area.
- **Scope creep.** Be careful to stay within the remit of the job or contract and don't randomly add extra tasks or outcomes without proper preparation or training. For example, don't get your bookkeeper to do sales calls just because they have time!
- **Interfering**. Remember the old adage 'Don't buy a dog and bark yourself'. You are hiring them for their expertise – don't start second guessing them unless you have serious concerns about their competence.

A really good time management tip from Brian Tracy. Delegate as much as you can as obviously this frees up your time.

If any of the activities are to be done by others it is important to make sure that you have their commitment to the dates you need to be met. Conversations around this can mean that you have to move the end date of the goal because of other people's availability.

And if you are using other people to do things, then you may want to consider planning goals further ahead so you can guarantee they can fit in with your timetable. Don't assume other businesses will be there when you need them.

> *"Only do what only you can do."*
> **Sir John Harvey Jones quoting Paul Sloane**

The 7 Step Action Planning System to Achieve Any Goal

CHAPTER 8

H is for How Long

Before we can schedule the activities, we need to know how long each task is going to take.

When you first start putting together an action plan you may have no idea how long it will take. Rather than spending too much time on trying to work it out I recommend you guess. (Or you may have a good handle on this.)

Going forward get into the habit of noting how long things take so you can do this part of the process more effectively and can spot opportunities for improving the processes.

Generally, I find people are a bit optimistic as to how quickly they can get things done!

Run through all the tasks and estimate how long each is likely to take and write it on the post-it notes or sheet of paper. This is the amount of 'effort' (the actual time required to work on the task), not the elapsed time, which could be days or weeks if you spread the effort out.

How accurate are you trying to be? The time is only an estimate so parts of days might be good enough. Would using hours be better? Try it and see.

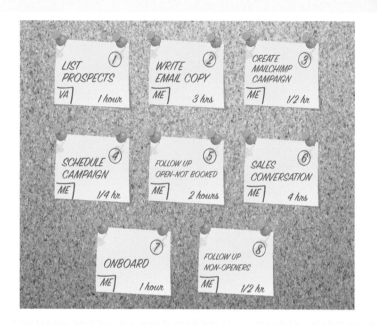

 Once you have an estimated time on each activity then add up the total time for each, concentrating solely on your own tasks.

Does the goal still look sensible given the time needed? If not adjust the goal or the timeline.

> "Estimating is what you do when you don't know."
>
> Sherman Kent

CHAPTER 9

A is for Allocate

Now all the preparation is done you are ready to drop this all into the planning template.

30 Day Plan Template

30 DAY GOAL		
Notes: The goal should be specific, measurable, achievable, relevant and timely. It should move the business forward and not simply be something off the To Do list		
Week commencing:	Who	Steps to be taken:
Week commencing:	Who	Steps to be taken:
Week commencing:	Who	Steps to be taken:
Week commencing:	Who	Steps to be taken:

The 30 Day Plan template is on page 10 of the GALAHAD Workbook

Step 1 – Add the dates

Decide whether you are using 'week commencing' or 'week ending' dates and add in the dates for each week. When I do this with members it is driven by when in the week we are having our training session.

Step 2 – Write the goal

Write the 30-day goal at the top of the planning template. Remember to check it against the SMART criteria if you haven't already done so.

Step 3 – Sanity check

Before allocating the activities to the 4 or 5 weeks of the 30-day plan make sure you have accounted for things that are already committed. It might be that some weeks have no capacity for working on your strategic goal. (That is fine.)

Step 4 – Plan the activities

Allocate the activities to each of the weeks using either the numbers you previously wrote on the post-it notes/sheet or the descriptions if that works better for you. Start with the last week first and then work backwards towards the first week.

Step 5 – Review the goal – adjust if necessary

Once you have allocated the activities it will be obvious if you have tried to put too much into the 30 days as you will have post-it notes left over that cannot be put into week 1.

In this case, there are several things you can do.

- Change the goal for the 30 days by creating an interim milestone;

- Make the 30-day goal a 35-day goal, for example;

- Revisit the diary commitments for priority and see if some can be moved so there is time to complete the goal.

30 Day Plan Template

30 DAY GOAL	Onboard 3 clients at a monthly revenue of £2500 each and generate 10 leads to convert to clients in December

Notes: The goal should be specific, measurable, achievable, relevant and timely. It should move the business forward and not simply be something off the To Do list

Week commencing:	Who	Steps to be taken:
7 Sep 20xx	Virtual Assistant	1
Week commencing:	Who	Steps to be taken:
14 Sep 20xx	Me	2 and 3
Week commencing:	Who	Steps to be taken:
21 Sep 20xx	Me	4, 5 and 6
Week commencing:	Who	Steps to be taken:
28 Sep 20xx	Me	7 and 8

> "A plan is what, a schedule is when. It takes both a plan and a schedule to get things done."
>
> Peter Turla

The 30 Day Plan template is on page 9 of the GALAHAD Workbook

CHAPTER 10

D is for Diarise - The Final Piece of the Puzzle

So, what is the final part of the puzzle? It is very simple but very powerful. It is to book the activities into your diary as *meetings with yourself.*

So 'D' is for 'DIARISE'.

These meetings should carry **the same level of importance as any client meeting** and should only be moved under exceptional circumstances.

This is all about planning time with intent. For these meetings turn off all notifications, phones etc. and get really focused on the task. Give it 100% of your attention and keep going until it is done.

Be aware of the items you are likely to procrastinate on. Commit fully to the meeting in your diary and think about what time of day you might want to book in the more difficult things. Think about why you might be procrastinating.

If you have trouble overcoming this, then consider the effect of not getting the action done and therefore not delivering the 30-day goal – how would that feel? Create pain to encourage action!

Take each activity and book it into your diary.

When looking at when in the week an activity can be performed, consider what time of day works best for you for that sort of activity and use those slots for strategic action.

Make sure you consider bank holidays, half terms, family events and other business priorities. It can be hard to get the right level of focus during these times.

> "The key is not to prioritize what's on your schedule, but to schedule your priorities."
>
> Stephen Covey

CHAPTER 11

Why There Is One More Thing You *Must* Do

As you and I know action plans don't stand still. As you complete the steps that make up each action you will learn things and other factors will come into play.

Stuff happens!

So, once the 7 steps of GALAHAD are complete and the action plan has been started the next really important thing is the **REVIEW**. Develop a process for review and adjustment for your business that fits into your working time.

Peter Drucker said *'What gets measured, gets managed'*.

Along with booking the plan activities into the diary the review also needs to be booked in. The first thing to decide is how often and when you are going to do the review. Do you already have a regular review time where you look back over the preceding days and what has been done? Perhaps you could add the action plan review into this existing process.

Do you want to have an end of day review, end of week, halfway through the action plan? For the 30 day plan you might want to have a review on the days you have booked tasks. What works best for you and which will be most effective? The aim of the review is not only to measure progress. It is also to adjust the next set of activities with the aim of still completing the goal by the end of, in this case, the 30-day timeline.

Be aware that you cannot take responsibility for the outcome but only for the actions that lead towards it.

As with the activities, when it comes time to do the review, get really focused on the process. Ask yourself the following questions:

- Did the activity deliver what was needed? If not, why not?
- How can you improve its effectiveness?
- Did the time slot in the diary for the activity get hijacked?
- Why did that happen?
- Where can you book it back in?
- How do you reduce the chances of future hijacks?

Review Template

Activity Number	Achieved?	What went well?	What could be improved?	What will I change next time?

The Reviewing template is on page 11 of the GALAHAD Workbook

The 7 Step Action Planning System to Achieve Any Goal ▪

ill in the Review Template

On the template either repeat the post-it note reference number or the activity description. For the activities that were attempted assess whether the outcome of the activity was achieved or not. Were some partially achieved?

For those partially achieved what was the gap between desired outcome and actual? For those not achieved why was this?

Then think about what could be improved for each activity were it to be repeated. (Don't spend time on this for activities that are unique to this one action plan.) Add in what you will do differently next time.

Review Example

Activity Number	Achieved?	What went well?	What could be improved?	What will I change next time?
1	Yes	Ease of filtering the data to find the prospects	Need to tighten up the segmentation – one category is too wide	Update the data and resegment before running again
2	Yes	Full set of copy, headlines, subhead and image delivered on time	Need more subject lines to allow split testing	Split test subject lines
3	Yes	Went to plan	Further automation at some point	Nothing
4	Yes	Went out on time	Was it the best time to send?	Change send time and measure results
5	No	N/A	Need to get this better scheduled as the calls were overtaken by other things	Do them
6	Yes	The script used for the conversation flowed better and the offering made more sense	Close needs tightening	Rewrite the close and practice the new words
7	Yes	Initial onboarding steps worked well	There are a couple of the steps that are out of order/take too long	Reorder process and streamline
8	Yes	Easy to schedule in Mailchimp	Open rate	Test different hero image

For those activities that were not fully achieved or those that were hijacked, readjust the activities for the rest of the action plan period and adjust the diary to reflect those changes. If there is no capacity to pick up what didn't get done, then the target date for the plan may need to be slipped. What would be the impact of this? Are there other things that could be dropped in order to accommodate the remaining activities and reach that 30-day goal on time?

Find whatever mechanism works best for you to conduct and record the review. Some people really like a piece of paper or you may have an app (which can then send you automatic reminders).

Always measure by how far you have come – not how far there still is to go. Reward yourself for reaching milestones – avoid beating yourself up if you don't get quite there!

"Allow yourself to be proud of yourself and all the progress you've made. Especially the progress that no one else can see."

Anonymous

CHAPTER 12

You've Got This!

So, you now have amazing goals and ideas about where you want to take your business and what you want to achieve. But it seems impossible, or you are simply not making any progress.

As discussed, action plans are a huge part of achieving success – if you don't take action nothing happens.

The difference now is that you have a *clear action plan*. The first milestone for your initial goal is decided and you know what steps to take.

Done and dusted then? Maybe not quite.

As you and I know even if we have done all the preparation work, followed a process and planned in the actions, sometimes it is still hard to make it happen.

Here are some techniques to help you maintain momentum.

THE LETTER FROM THE FUTURE

You can strengthen the likelihood of achieving your vision with a 'letter from the future'. This technique helps you achieve goals and works on the principle that your subconscious does not know the difference between reality and imagination. If you tell it something 'is', it will work towards that being true.

Write a letter to a friend as if it is written in 3 years time. *'Hey, can you believe it's already 20XX'*. Describe how the day is, making sure you include the feelings and emotions you'll be experiencing. Use all your senses - what do you hear, smell, feel and see?

Tell them about the goals you've achieved in those 3 years - it's important to write as though the goals have been successfully attained. "A few months ago we signed up new customer one thousand - I am so proud to have reached this number. Yesterday I moved the family into the new house... the view from the terrace is every bit as wonderful as I thought." or "We hit our profit targets for the third year, and as I promised myself, the new car is outside. I took it out for a drive earlier - the smell of new leather and the smooth power under the bonnet made me feel a million dollars."

Think about how having that goal achieved will make you feel. Are you excited? Proud?

It is very important to include emotions and senses. It really embeds the belief you're already there and sets your subconcious on the hunt for what you've imagined.

VISUALISATION

Put together a set of images, or written notes, describing your goals. Put them somewhere you can see them every day. The more you relate to the images the more impactful they will be. At NASA when they were working on the project to get a man to the moon, they made simple signs saying, 'The Moon' and put them up all round Mission Control.

In the *Knowledge Vault* on page 74 I have included the link to a video from dressage rider Olivia Towers. Take a look. While this is aimed at riding a dressage test, the principle can be applied to your business goals, a sales conversation, and a telephone call – basically anything.

THE DREAM JAR

To help keep her motivated Carrie Green, founder of the *Female Entrepreneur Association*, uses a dream jar.

Grab a piece of paper, a pen, and a jar of any kind. Write down every goal and dream you have for the next 12 months. Business-related, personal, whatever you want for yourself in the next year, no matter how crazy or huge they may be – a key part of this exercise is that you're not allowed to limit yourself!

Once you've got your list, cut the paper up so that each goal is on its own strip. Fold them up and place them in your jar.

Pull one piece of paper from your dream jar every day. Take at least one minute to vividly visualise yourself achieving it. If you have enough time, 5-10 minutes is even more powerful!

> *"Where focus goes energy flows."*
>
> Tony Robbins

The 7 Step Action Planning System to **Achieve Any Goal** ■

CHAPTER 13

Summing Up

I believe that action plans are one of the things that businesses avoid at their peril. Benjamin Franklin said, *"If you fail to plan, you are planning to fail"*. But without action, a plan is only 'shelf-ware'.

Decide - today - that you are going to act on your business. Some of it will work, some won't, but doing nothing is really not an option. It is one of those 'simple - not easy' things.

- Use our GALAHAD process for your action planning
  - Goals
  - Activities
  - Logical Order
  - Assign
  - How long
  - Allocate
  - Diarise

- Once you have written the goal, test it against the SMART criteria. Does it need tightening up? Is it too big for the period you are looking at?

- Check each activity is totally relevant to the goal. The acid test is 'Does the activity move towards the goal'?

- Challenge the 'Who'. Does it have to be you? Can you delegate or outsource?

- Only have a couple of actions each week. Any more and it increases the likelihood of not achieving the tasks and we want to set the action plan up for success, not failure. Better to have small but achievable steps giving slow but steady progress rather than a long list that overwhelms.

- If you need several action plans running concurrently, how can you schedule the committed time to deliver them all?

- Build in reviews and measure results frequently.

- Be honest with yourself about which of the activities you are likely to procrastinate on and handle accordingly.

> *"All our dreams can come true if we have the courage to pursue them."*
>
> Walt Disney

Resourcing Activities

Remember firstly eliminate, then automate, then delegate.

- **Elimination** - if you don't need to do it, dump it
- **Automation** - is there an app or software that does it?
- **Delegation** - who can help you?

    Some possible resources for the remaining tasks:

    – Company or freelancer who has the 'specialist' skills needed, such as a VA or bookkeeper
    – Employee – existing team members
    – Professional
    – Casual employee
    – Mastermind group/Boardroom group
    – Volunteers
    – Intern
    – Work experience
    – Apprentice
    – Students
    – PeoplePerHour/Guru/Fiverr/Upwork
    – Copify
    – Design Pickle
    – Partner

The 7 Step Action Planning System to Achieve Any Goal ■

Longer Term Goals – Split Them Down

It's important to split larger goals into their 90 day tranches and then into 30 day milestones. I highlighted this in Chapter 5, and wanted to include some examples to demonstrate how this can be done.

For financial numbers this is relatively easy to do if you use just a straight line approach but for other goals it can be trickier.

On the following four pages are examples of how to split *Vision Roadmap* goals into manageable chunks. The examples cover products and services; number of customers; number of staff; and days worked per week.

Your labels on the spokes, or your routes to their achievement may be different, but the examples will show you ways you can break each goal down.

1. PRODUCTS AND SERVICES

This example shows a potential breakdown for expansion of your products and services.

It assumes that this business is aiming to add 10 products to their range in 3 years, then maps the key actions needed to reach a 90 day target.

Your goals may be about new products, additional services, or an expansion of your existing service. Adjust to suit your business aims.

VISION ROADMAP SPOKE: Products and Services

3 YEAR GOAL 10 new products

2 YEAR GOAL 4 new products

1 YEAR GOAL 2 new products

90 DAY TARGET 1 new product

MONTH 1: KEY ACTION

• Revisit customer pains, gains and jobs to be done and identify where the next new product could add most value. Validated with Market Research and customer surveys
• Confirm customer avatar within segment and identify cross sell opportunities

MONTH 2 – KEY ACTION

• Develop product value proposition, price point and define launch plan including social media, PR etc.
• Define key measures for effectiveness of marketing activities
• Review sales and delivery processes to make sure they fit new product

MONTH 3 – KEY ACTION

• Complete preparation of product and implement marketing plan
• Measure effectiveness of marketing and adjust as necessary

---

2. NUMBER OF CUSTOMERS

This will vary hugely depending on what sort of product or service you offer. Your time may be filled with just 5 new clients. Or you may be able to provide your product to thousands.

Again, set targets that are appropriate for you. Don't be afraid to make them a stretch. They should be ambitious, but flexible.

Once you have the actions decided for month 1, you have the goals for your first GALAHAD 30 day plan.

VISION ROADMAP SPOKE: Number of Customers

3 YEAR GOAL 300 extra

2 YEAR GOAL 100 extra

1 YEAR GOAL 50 extra

90 DAY TARGET 25 extra

MONTH 1: KEY ACTION

- Review data on where clients come from and the related conversion rates
- Segment red hot v warm v cold prospects
- Focus on best channels. Define the key messages for the prime segment to generate new leads and set up marketing campaign or similar

MONTH 2 – KEY ACTION

- Follow up on all leads generated
- Keep a check on conversion rates and aim to improve
- Current target – to get 25 new customers need 100 leads

MONTH 3 – KEY ACTION

- Close deals with new customers and make sure delivery exceeds expectations.
- Ask them for referrals

---

3. NUMBER OF STAFF

For you this might be staff, or contractors who can take care of the aspects of your business you don't *have* to do.

This could be a bookkeeper or accountant, digital marketing expert, office manager, sales team... as your business grows, the people you need to help you become more important.

If you do your own books at the moment, that's time you don't need to spend. A part-time employee or contractor to take care of the accounts could be your first 90 day goal.

VISION ROADMAP SPOKE: Number of staff

3 YEAR GOAL 4 FTE

2 YEAR GOAL 2 FTE

1 YEAR GOAL 1 FTE

90 DAY TARGET Have roles and skills identified for first person

MONTH 1: KEY ACTION

• Revisit process skills template and identify which tasks in which processes have the greatest opportunity cost and do not have to be done by owner

MONTH 2 – KEY ACTION

• Work out what the key inputs of skills, knowledge etc. for the step are based on the Kipling questions

MONTH 3 – KEY ACTION

• Write roles and responsibilities to include skills requirements ready to advertise or give to an HR agency
• Include factors such as full or part time; employed or supplier; location base and of course remuneration.

---

4. DAYS WORKED PER WEEK

Quality of life delivered by your business may be one of your key goals. More time with your family, more holiday, more opportunities to work on other projects.

What would need to be in place to allow you to walk away from the office a day or more a week? Who would you need in place to keep things ticking over?

Maybe you want to work remotely, travelling the world and running your business from a laptop. What would make that possible?

VISION ROADMAP SPOKE: Days worked per week

3 YEAR GOAL 3

1 YEAR GOAL 4

6 MTH GOAL 4

90 DAY TARGET Have sales process defined and outsourced

MONTH 1: KEY ACTION

• Document the sales process

MONTH 2 – KEY ACTION

• Using the Process Skills Template see which steps can be outsourced or reassigned

MONTH 3 – KEY ACTION

• Implement outsource/reassignment

Knowledge Vault

Welcome to the Knowledge Vault. Here you can find some information resources related to the action-taking part of your business.

THINGS TO WATCH

Olivia Towers Visualisation (excuse the Ads)
http://bit.ly/TBKitch2

Simon Sinek TED Talk
http://bit.ly/TBKitch3

THINGS TO READ

Simon Sinek - *Start with Why*

Brian Tracy - *Eat that Frog*

THINGS TO EXPLORE

Organising your activities

Bullet journals (You can get the physical journals from a number of places or just use a dot printed notebook)
http://bit.ly/TBKitch6

Best self-journal
http://bit.ly/TBKitch8

Trello (boards and lists to help you get organised – it's good for collaboration too)
http://bit.ly/TBkitch4

Asana (organise projects and teams) http://bit.ly/TBKitch5

Todoist (iPhone organiser app) http://bit.ly/TBKitch7

FINDING RESOURCES

People Per Hour
http://bit.ly/TBKitch9

Guru
http://bit.ly/TBKitch10

Fiverr
www.fiverr.com

Upwork
http://bit.ly/TBKitch12

Copify (Copywriting service)
http://bit.ly/TBKitch13

Design Pickle (Graphic Design service)
http://bit.ly/TBKitch14

Dear Reader...

If you have made it to this page then congratulations! You have completed your very first 30-day action plan and I wish you every success with implementing it and achieving the results you desire. Time to celebrate and reward yourself.

I hope you have enjoyed learning and practicing the GALAHAD system. You now have in your tool kit a method of aceing action plans every time you need to.

The Business Kitchen's mission is to provide the training, skills and knowledge for small business owners, like you, to help you overcome your business challenges and achieve your long term business goals.

To find out more about my online membership and how it can help you work on your business please visit:

http://bit.ly/TBKitch1

Or email me **gill@thebusinesskitchen.net**

About the Author

Gill Smith co-founded The Business Kitchen in 2014 with then business partner, Nigel Knowlman. With similar city and corporate backgrounds, and a shared interest in how small and medium-sized businesses operated, they joined forces. Their aim? To bring big firm consultancy skills to smaller businesses with a desire to grow.

They started a training company, and set up a membership that provided a series of practical, face-to-face training sessions. Members would not only learn from Nigel and Gill but from the rest of the group. The main focus of the Business Kitchen's training was working 'on' the business. The processes and mechanics of running and directing a successful enterprise.

Members loved the training and fully acknowledged the value of what they were learning. But most of them were having real trouble finding the time and energy to apply it. Gill realised that something was missing – a critical system that would help busy business owners set aside time for steering their companies – and act on it.

GALAHAD was born.

Early in 2020, Nigel retired, leaving Gill at the helm. Changing circumstances often lead to fresh ideas, and GALAHAD is Gill's first major launch. Business owners can't work 'on' their business if they struggle with why or how they should. GALAHAD makes it clear, and makes it simple. It's key to getting stuff done.

That's why Gill calls it her Spearhead product.

The Business Kitchen now has over 70 members and has helped over 700 businesses via one off workshops and events. Gill is now expanding her reach to allow her to help many more business people who want to know how to ensure success and secure their future.

Testimonials

Many of the following testimonials were given by business people who attended Gill's face-to-face GALAHAD workshop. The steps they worked through are the same as those described in this book.

f you'd like to attend the next workshop and work through your action plan live with Gill, get in touch and ask for an invite to attend.

gill@thebusinesskitchen.net

"I have attended two of Gill online workshops and she is fabulous to work with. Engaging, well prepared and informative. On both occasions I arrived with a confusing muddle in my head and left with a written action plan and clarity about how to start work. I highly recommend a call or workshop with Gill."

"I know that action planning feels like it should be common sense...and in so many ways it is. The reason you should attend this workshop is because it takes what you are instinctively capable of and creates a framework that makes your planning almost foolproof, and forces you to create the time you need to make it work."

"Well worth the time for any new or established business."

"Very useful. Great to create some space to think. Useful exercise – helped me realise I could apply this approach to other goals."

Testimonials

"You will learn a valuable way of creating an action plan – chaotic thoughts and ideas will become a manageable plan."

"Very useful. Simple steps that clear your mind."

"A great insight into how to help structure your idea and understand next steps."

"Really, unless you are making too much money, working too few hours, and finding life kicking along too smoothly, I would recommend it to any small business owner."

"Made us to get to where we are quicker, it's been fantastic, a really good experience."

"Well worth the time if you want to take your business seriously."

Testimonials

"There is a real mix between inspiring big, ambitious thinking and then also getting down to the details of how to achieve this. Lots of practical ideas to start working on straight away in your business. The team understand the reality of running a small business or being a sole trader yet still encourage planning for a bigger picture in the future - whatever that means to you."

"You'll come out with an increased sense of motivation and confidence that you can achieve!"

"Gill your excellent online training to create a 30-day Action Plan was packed with great advice and practical tools to enable us to create a structured, focused plan during the Zoom. I now feel on track to create success by 'treating my business with the respect it deserves'. From now on I shall also be diarising meetings with myself - excellent tip! Thank you!"

ACCESSING THE WORKBOOK

You can download the workbook from this URL:

http://bit.ly/galahadworkbook

Or scan this QR code to go straight to the download site.

The workbook can be used online or in print.

If you want to print it out, I recommend you select pages **3 to 12** as the cover will use up a lot of ink!